WHO THE *f*ck* AM I TO BE A COACH?!

A Warrior's Guide to Building a Wildly Successful
Coaching Business From the Inside Out

MEGAN JO WILSON

Difference Press

McLean, Virginia, USA

Difference Press is a trademark of Becoming Journey, LLC

Published 2017

ISBN: 978-1-68309-223-0

DISCLAIMER

Cover Design: Jennifer Stimson

Editing: Anna Paradox

Author photo courtesy of Shoshannah White and Tonee Harbert

ADVANCE PRAISE

"If you know that you are called to be a coach, but you don't know an authentic way to start, this book is for you! It includes inspiring stories and practical advice, all while staying strongly connected to the power of spirit and inspiration."

–L.A. REDING,
Master Certified Coach

"Megan Jo is a gifted, amazing, and powerful woman, coach, and leader! I was blessed to be in her presence during my Co-Active coaches' training and I am the better for it! For those who cannot experience her in person, this book is the next best option! Enjoy!"

–DENEEN BENNETT,
Owner, KDB Couture Consulting, LLC

"As a newbie to coaching, Megan Jo's book felt like a love letter to ME! Practical advice, helpful hints, and useful examples all rolled into one easy-to-read book. Every coach should have this on his or her required reading list!"

–EMILY COHEN,
Author of *From Generation to Generation*

"As an artist, I felt completely inspired by Megan Jo's words to move forward and succeed. Through the doubt, fear, joy, and most certainly through the celebration – this book will help you find your way."

–SARA HALLIE RICHARDSON,
Singer, Songwriter, Producer

"Written in an authentic, beautiful, irreverent voice, *Who the F*ck Am I to Be a Coach?!* captures the exact fears and discomforts many of my clients share as they face the rollercoaster of entrepreneurship. The book leads the new coach through concrete steps (and the very real emotional responses) to building a successful business in a non-traditional field. A great read!"

–LIZ LAJOIE,
The Coaches' CFO

"If you've wanted to launch a successful coaching business but haven't known where to start, you will LOVE this book. Megan Jo gives you the foundation of who you need to BE and what you need to DO to make your dream a reality. Finally, a business book that encourages you to build a wildly successful coaching business and have a great time doing it!"

–ERICA ROSS KRIEGER,
M.A., BCC Business and Life Coach

DEDICATION

For Bonnie Cohen.

My first and forever Fairy Godmother who reminded me
again and again that life is magical.

TABLE OF CONTENTS

INTRODUCTION

Hi, brave human.

I see you.

I see you sitting at your computer. You scheduled Fridays to see clients because you know you are called to be a coach, but you don't actually *have* any clients in your calendar, so you are sitting at your computer wondering why you don't have clients, and wondering how the hell to find them. Wondering what your brand is.... And what about a niche? And how does MailChimp work?

You're frustrated because no one ever really told you it would be this hard to get clients and start a real coaching business.

But you're a smart cookie so you think, Maybe there's a webinar about it. Yep there's one. And there's another one. Are these for real? you wonder. Oh god, she's *gorgeous. Look at* those red lips. Her website is perfect. She has 500 people in her workshop! Oh my god she *has 586,000 followers! I need to work harder. I need structure. Maybe I need a virtual assistant. I'm going to look into that. Or should I start with a logo? How do I describe what coaching is on an elevator and...*

Where's the magic that I felt in class? Am I really called to this coaching thing or was I just inspired for a hot minute?

What am I doing wrong?

Stuck in Overwhelm

I know this story because I have coached hundreds of people through it. I also lived it. I knew that coaching was my calling, and then painfully realized that I had no idea how to turn it into a successful career, and doubted my ability to pull it off successfully. You are also called. You know that this is what you were born to do. When you're coaching – even when it's not your best coaching – it just feels right. And going through the coach training, working with others who crave connection and challenge, and feeling all the deep feelings, is like being with others who finally understand you and speak your language.

But a day or a maybe a week later, as you step away from the classroom and return to "real life," you feel lost. You become suffocated by the feeling that you have no idea how to make this dream of building a real coaching business a reality. You don't know how to attract clients (not to mention how to charge money for coaching – Lord please!) even though you kinda feel like you should. You find yourself stuck and overwhelmed and... not coaching anyone.

Now not only is your dream not being realized, but you feel guilty for not realizing your dream! You're in the dream-making business after all, so on top of all of this, you feel like a fraud. You're not changing lives and you're not supporting clients, and of course, you're not generating any income. This beautiful dream – that looked so rich and so powerful in the land of your imagination – feels so dreadfully far away back here on earth as you sit at your computer... staring at Facebook... and hating it.

What's at Stake?

As a coach, you have incredible gifts to share and you know it. You have the power to change lives and you know it. Your spirit has been called to be a coach and you know it. And you also know that, in order to share your gift in a powerful way, you are going to have to build a sustainable and profitable business.

Here's what's also true: If you try to build your business from a place of fear and self-doubt, it won't be sustainable. If you treat your gifts lightly and forget to enjoy the ride, your business won't be sustainable. And without a doubt, if you don't find a way to make your business profitable, it won't be sustainable.

And what a shame that would truly be. Because your clients need you. They are out there in the world right now waiting for *you* – not me and not the woman you envy on Facebook. They want to work with you and right now they don't know how to find you, hire you, and get started.

So, you're not serving yourself and you're not serving your clients and it's kinda... half-baked. You know how it is when you make brownies but the toothpick comes out with chocolate goop on it? That shit is half-baked, but you're still trying to cut them into squares and tell yourself it's all good. But it's not all good. You deserve *so much more*. It's time to have the fully baked brownies with that crusty edge – and still warm and chewy inside – and maybe some fresh whipped cream and vanilla ice-cream and chocolate syrup with the tiniest pinch of sea salt on top. That's what you deserve. A brownie sundae kind of life!

Building a Business from the Inside Out

I know this is not the first book you've ever picked up with a dream that it could change your life for good. There are hundreds of books for coaches, and even more courses, workbooks, webinars, and business seminars. I, myself, have five bookcases full of books designed to help me get unstuck in my business, my money, and my relationships.

But none of the books I've ever checked out have reflected to me what my *soul* knows. None of them say, "Before you do anything in your business, make sure you feel good." Go feel good. *Then* think about your niche, your budget, and your elevator speech. Start with feeling really good about your own life so that you can serve other people to feel good, too.

I want you to commit so profoundly to your own fulfillment and self-love – even and especially when it comes to building your coaching business – that you end up appreciating every single step of the journey. My wish is that you take a stand against a culture that screams "You're not good enough," and claim with every fiber of your being "Fuck yes, I am."

As we claim our power from the inside, a surprising thing happens on the outside. We find instead of becoming more self-absorbed, we become more and more interested in serving *others*. We care less about what other people think of us. We care less about doing it perfectly and we care more about choosing *who* we will be and *how* we will be, and what our impact will be while we're here. From this place, you will touch hundreds and maybe thousands of lives, because you have committed to being more and more of the amazing and brave human you were created to be.

This is the path of the warrior. This is not *always* the easy path or the fun path (except when it is and – man oh man – it is so worth it!) and that's why not everyone takes it. It requires courage and commitment and a whole lot of faith. Others may not understand what you are doing and they may not like it, and let's be honest, there are parts *of you* that may not like it.

So I understand that a part of you might be feeling a little bit nervous and wondering right now if you have what it takes to go all in with living your purpose as a coach. But there is another part of you that knows you have everything you need. This is the warrior. Let's listen to *that* part of you.

Fear or Faith

Carolyn Myss writes, "Any choice made from fear is a violation of the energy of faith," and I know this to be true in all areas of life – and certainly when we're becoming the person who commits to building a successful coaching business. When you have the space to take a big long sip of faith, you will find that your fears begin to dissolve, and the fog clears, and your purpose-filled priorities begin to make their way into your daily routines. You find yourself enjoying the process more, and, as you enjoy the process, miraculous coincidences begin to bloom all around you.

What will your business be like when you put down your fear and step into faith? When you put your own joy and inspiration first? When will you commit fully to your success and listen – and respond – to divine guidance at every step of the way?

Don't get it twisted. In this place, the actions you will take *are* real and required. This is not the land of meditating and then clicking your heels together and praying that clients will start calling you out of the blue and your taxes will get paid by a magical yellow fairy. In the real world of running a real, successful business, you *will* pay the taxes, and you *will* build the website (or the right person will come along to help you pay the taxes and build the website) but you will do it from a place of faith and abundance rather than a place of fear and anxiety.

Nothing Matters More Than Feeling Good

As coaches, it is our responsibility to make feeling good a top priority. Good can mean a lot of things. Good can mean inspired, awake, alive, fulfilled, content, proud, joyful, excited. It can even feel exhilarating and terrifying (which is why we jump out of planes and ride roller coasters – I mean *really*?!)

I know for sure that feeling good *does not* mean feeling anxious, numb, depressed, less-than, or shut down. I know for sure that it *is* possible to build a strategic and successful coaching business that is built on a foundation of faith, confidence, and inspiration. How? This book will show you the way.

I have worked with hundreds and hundreds of clients who are coaches themselves, and have seen a powerful pattern emerge as they committed to building a wildly successful coaching business. This pattern informed a framework of attitudes, perspectives, and practical tools that I now bring to all of my clients who are spiritual entrepreneurs on a mission to become the warrior coaches they were born to be so that they can serve their clients and transform lives.

Each chapter in this book frames these concepts and tools in a way that I pray is clear, impactful, and useful. Most of the chapters also include exercises for you to take out of the book and into your own life if you are willing to engage, underline, act, and reflect.

It's not an accident that you found this book. There are no accidents. Some part of you is ready to start this journey in a whole new way and I am in your corner – ready with a warm towel and a bottle of water (or is it red wine?). In any case, here I am with my hand on your back.

Let's do this.

THE COACH'S CALLING

"Everything depends on a person's courage to trust that she can handle whatever happens after she – the dreamer – commits to the aliveness of the unknown."

–MILNE KINTNER, LIFE COACH

I discovered coaching in 2004. I was a 27-year-old musician, farmer, and salad cook with a long dirty blonde braid and strong tan arms. My big brother gave me a gift certificate to a coaching class at an organization called CTI. I had no idea what coaching was, but he assured me that I was a natural, and that I shouldn't let my "gremlins" get in the way of my dreams... whatever that meant.

At the end of the third day in this first coaching class, I had one of the most profound spiritual experiences of my life. As we circled up in our chairs to say our final words to complete the experience, there was an electric chill running from my skull, down my spine, and through my fingertips. I had to lean over and put my forearms on my knees because I was so dizzy. I was overwhelmed at what I had just experienced and had powerful visions of how this model could transform the world. Not just my clients. Not just my community. The *world*. All I could say was, "This is very important work."

At that moment, I committed myself to being a "real coach" and making it my life's work. I was still working part-time as a cook, baker, farmer – busting my ass for 10 bucks an hour. I was coaching a handful of people, mostly friends of friends. In other words, I was coaching anyone who could put together a sentence, and charging $20 a session, and still felt like I was over-charging.

From Calling to Career

It turns out that what I was charging wasn't enough to keep me afloat. Money was getting tighter every month. But as I focused more on making money, I started to become self-conscious about my coaching. I crunched the numbers and knew that I needed to charge more, but as a "starving artist" and the youngest of five kids in a house where money was often tight, this was incredibly confronting for me.

I stopped coaching on the beach and started working on the phone. I stopped taking days off and started working harder on my website in order to get more clients. But, the harder I worked, the fewer clients I was enrolling. My budget got tighter and tighter as my enjoyment of coaching drifted away. The magic of the classroom was so very far away. I remember sitting with a prospective client in my tiny office with the butternut-squash colored walls, and as they spoke, all I could think was, "If they sign up, I'll have half of my office rent. If they don't sign up, I'm financially fucked."

They didn't sign up.

As the joy and faith in myself and my coaching became dehydrated by the invisible but ever-present pressure to build a "real" business, I watched my income and my clients come to a slow and painful halt. Like someone riding a bike on smooth tarmac and then hitting sand, I just couldn't peddle anymore. I felt like a fraud and wanted to give up.

When You're Called to Be a Coach

When I look back at my coaching journey over the years, the pattern I see is clear: Every time I lost track of my own fulfillment and my deep knowing that this was my calling, my business would suffer. And every time I would recover my own sense of my big purpose and my faith, the business would begin to grow with ease.

When I stopped enjoying my life, the clients evaporated. When I stopped walking in the woods, my coaching sessions would become flat and formulaic. When I neglected to take a break from the frantic pace of life to just feel a sense of gratitude for what I already had, the opportunities for new business seemed to disappear.

So I started making my own fulfillment my top priority. I started to pray more and sing more and savor the meal more – even when it was ramen with a hard-boiled egg, chopped scallions and some cheap white wine. When I felt better about myself, I was able to commit to the journey, even when I knew it would be challenging. When I felt connected to divine guidance, the aliveness and passion would return to my coaching sessions.

I continued to honor my spiritual side more fully, seeking out joy and pleasure and inspiration as if it was my most important job, *and from that place,* I began to become more conscious about my relationship to money and filled in the gaps of my knowledge around niche, marketing, pricing, and enrolling the clients that I was called to serve. Things shifted very quickly.

Being a "Real Coach"

As a coach trainer, I get to meet the most incredible, courageous, heart-centered, passionate people in the world. During each and every three-day intensive training, I watch these amazing people blossom into powerful and effective coaches.

Sadly, when I follow-up with many of these coaches to see how they are doing and how many clients they have, they often say they're *not coaching*! When I ask them why, here are the most typical responses:

"I don't know how to get clients."

"I don't know how much to charge."

"I think I need more training."

"I don't have a website yet."

"I need to have a blog."

"I don't have a niche. (I don't think I want to limit myself like that.)"

"I don't really know how to explain the value of coaching."

Although I completely understand this, it totally breaks my heart! You're learning to be a coach and doing your best to learn what it takes to launch a successful business, and these are all new skills, so of course you are facing so many of your inner doubts and fears! But what a waste of an amazing gift! What a loss for the clients that could be served! This is why I have committed myself to supporting you.

You are not crazy for feeling overwhelmed by all the training options out there, and you are not a fraud for doubting your ability to be a successful coach! It's normal for you to feel like you don't know what to do next.

It's my goal to connect you to knowing the amazing coach you already are, so that you can connect to your clients as soon as possible. When you are deeply connected to who you need to *be* to build this business, the doing becomes more effortless.

I'll never forget when my first coach Bonnie (who called herself a Fairy Godmother) said to me, "I built a successful business as a coach... and you can, too." Bonnie died last year, but she has a fierce spirit, so I invite you to hear her voice – and mine –circled around you. Hear us when we say:

"I built a successful business as a coach... and you can, too."

THE PATH OF THE WARRIOR

"A warrior begins to take responsibility for the direction of her life."

–PEMA CHODRON, *THE PLACES THAT SCARE YOU: A GUIDE TO FEARLESSNESS IN DIFFICULT TIMES*

The framework you're about to read is designed to support you in committing joyfully and courageously to becoming the coach and the leader you were born to be.

My ultimate goal is for you to be able to say with confidence, "I'm ready to start working with clients now. I am awake to my purpose, and I am willing to learn. I am willing to dream big. I am willing to serve."

When you are connected to this space, you ram an energetic stake in the ground that's like a sonic boom to the universe that says, "I am open. I am here to be used." And she will respond in kind.

Here's what's coming in the following chapters:

Gratitude

When gratitude is our starting point, everything changes. This is particularly true when we're stepping into something that triggers anxiety, and believe me, building a business is not for the faint of heart. Gratitude is the antidote to anxiety. Gratitude is the balm for "I don't have enough and I am not enough." When we shift our attention to what we already have, and who we really are, we realize that we are already rich beyond measure, and that we have something unique and valuable to offer. Do not underestimate this as a foundational building block. You will not build a successful coaching business if you feel like shit (believe me, I've tried). Build your business from a place of gratitude for who you are, and what you have, and you will be amazed at what unfolds.

Vision

The power of big vision is radically under-utilized in our culture, but it is truly one of the most miraculous tools I've ever seen at work. I have vision boards that I could show you from ten years ago that are a perfect reflection of my current reality. You must utilize your vision, meaning that you must constantly leverage it as a source of inspiration to pull you through the muck and mire of bringing our spiritual dreams into the mundane world. You must be intimately connected with your Future Self –the part of you that *already has* the successful coaching business.

Your big vision will also include financial freedom, which can be a confronting subject for many new coaches. This chapter will explain why it is critical to get into a conscious relationship with money so that you can build a sustainable business that will serve others for years to come.

Service

Do you know who you are called to serve? Do you know her pain and her dreams as intimately as you know your own? Are you relating to her every day in your prayers and in your marketing efforts? To build a successful coaching practice, you must intimately understand this client, and relate to her on *her* terms. She does not know what you know. She does not have the skills that you have. This chapter will help you define your client and her struggles so that you can find each other and make all the good things happen. When you know her and feel her pain, you can get over yourself and get to work.

Inspiration

Living your life inspired is a part of your job as a coach. You must be a model of the possibility of having an outrageously fulfilling life, despite the demon voices, internal and external, who say, "That's not realistic." "That's not responsible." Or my very least favorite, "That's not professional." You must stand as a beacon of hope for your clients. You must *be* the person your client is dying to hire. When you make your own inspiration a priority, you will find incredible sources of untapped energy. You will not feel groggy, or depressed, or numb when you are inspired. They just don't hang together.

Confidence

Our mind is such an amazing thing. It thinks between 50–70 thousand conscious thoughts a day – and those are just the conscious ones! The thoughts that we think over and over become our beliefs or what we "know" to be true. They therefore determine our sense of what is possible in our own (and, by the way, our clients') lives. We are not brought into this world believing that we are not good enough or that anything is impossible. (If you don't believe me, come hang out with my four-year-old.) We must re-order our thoughts so that we create the best possible conditions for our purpose to be fulfilled.

Commitment

Are you all in as a coach? Have you decided that this is your life's work even when it's hard? Even when you fail in public? Even when you're feeling stuck? What about when you succeed beyond your wildest dreams? Being a professional coach can look so many different ways, and the market is only expanding. You can make an amazing living and an amazing life as a coach, but you're going to have to put away your plan B and step fully into trusting yourself and your choice to go all in. This is going to be an incredible relief and will improve all of your results, and this chapter will show you why.

Courage

It is one thing to *long* for success (which is safer so most people stay here, saying, "I have *so much* potential...") and another thing entirely to move toward success (which is more confronting because here you find out what your potential actually is). Are you ready to be seen as an expert? To really find out what your potential really is? To fail and succeed beyond your wildest imagination? You might not be ready yet, and that's okay because you have what it takes. It takes a ton of courage and I know you have that because you are a warrior. You have wisdom to share and it's time to share it.

Grace

You know without knowing what grace is. You know what it's like when you are being directed by divine intention, and you know what it's like when you deny it. There are ways that we can "enter in" to grace – or deny it – and this is a critical choice on our journey to spiritual success as a coach. We must return again and again to grace, even when the world, our busy schedule, or our children are screaming against it.

GRATITUDE

"Without a mindset of gratitude, we will never appreciate what we have, and risk living a life yearning forever for what we don't have."

—DEBORAH COLMAN, LEADERSHIP COACH

This may be hard to believe, but you already have *everything you need,* and what's more, you are already living so many parts of your success story. You are surrounded by evidence of your success and brilliance, but your brain has what's called a "negativity bias" so it notices more of what's *not* working: How little money is in your bank account. How few clients you have. How much better *she* is doing with her on-line coaching business...

This sensitivity to the unpleasant gets particularly triggered when we are learning something new. I see lots of new coaches struggle with this in the classroom. They want to be the best coach in the world, and they want it *now*. It's wonderful to strive for excellence but not so wonderful when we kick the shit out of ourselves for not doing things perfectly from day one. This obsession with perfection is also cultural.

Do you turn on the television or scroll through social media to find a barrage of messages saying, "You're doing just fine! There's nothing to improve! Just keep enjoying the ride and you'll get there eventually!"

Not so much.

We value "more" and we value "faster." More money! More friends! More likes! More houses! And the more we feed this monster, the hungrier it gets.

So how can we keep ourselves feeling optimistic when we are learning to be a coach and living in a culture that is obsessed with improvement, striving, and being the best? I think my friend – and very successful coach – Eric says it best: "You gotta get really good at being bad." When we loosen the grip of perfectionism, we can swing out, take risks, play more, and handle the mess. This is the place of deep learning, real connection, and, in my experience – a whole hell of a lot of fun.

You Are Learning

Words are powerful, so whenever I hear my clients saying things like, "I hate marketing," or "I'm terrible with money," or "I suck at sales," I invite them to reframe their language in a more empowering way:

"I'm *learning* how to market my coaching."

"I'm *learning* how to be conscious with my money."

"I'm *learning* how to get good at sales in a way that works for me."

What's it like to be standing in the perspective of "I suck?" For me, even as I write, I can feel my jaw getting tighter.

My spine collapses. I am immediately anxious, jealous, and overwhelmed with all the things I need to get done *now*. I am not exaggerating. I can go there just as fast as you can. Let's not go there.

Now stand in "I'm learning." Can you feel the shift? Suddenly I'm not a terrible person for having some gaps in my knowledge. I can even appreciate all of the things I already know. There is a sense of progress being made and a deep knowing that I am on my way. My excitement goes up and my shoulders go down. What happens for you? Which perspective would serve you and your coaching business?

Creating a Calm Sea

One of my favorite teachers is Florence Scovel-Schinn. She was a Christian healer in the 1920s who was teaching "The Secret" long before it was trendy. She wrote, "My ships come in on a calm sea." The ships she is talking about are blessings, opportunities, relationships, and clients that are eager to find you. The calm sea is a faithful and relaxed attitude.

The more we scramble, the choppier the waters become, and the more difficult it is for our ships – our blessings – to arrive. In other words, when we are anxious, we are in a state of scarcity that cuts off the blessing. Instead we can find ways to shift our focus, shift our thoughts, so that we can relax into a state of delighted expectation *even when* it appears that things are falling apart.

This is not about pretending that everything is perfect or that there is no suffering in the world. This is about finding the value in every situation, every relationship, and every moment of our experience. This is about assuming that everything that comes our way is divinely ordained for our growth and fulfillment. This is about being present to the beauty, wonder, and abundance that can be found if we are willing to put our attention to it.

Redefining Success

My client Kathleen came to me because she knew I was a coach, but also an artist and professional performer. She and I had met in a creative non-fiction writing workshop in the woods of Maine, and connected instantly.

While I never did much with my memoir idea (a journal that detailed my adventures as a farmhand), Kathleen was fully committed to finishing her manuscript and getting it published, despite the fact that she was a single mother of a pre-teen daughter and a full time high school English teacher.

She came to me in despair. "I just don't know how to make the time to write this book. My life is a mess!"

"Look around the living room, what do you see?" I asked.

"My kitchen sink is full of dishes, I have toys all over the living room, and a pile of laundry the size of Mount

Katahdin. I told you my life is a mess!"

Me: "What is there to appreciate?"

Silence. (Maybe silent groans?)

Kathleen: "At least I'm writing."

Me: "You're writing your book! How brave! With all of the things you have going on, you're still writing a book."

Kathleen: (more hopeful) "That's true. And I know I am going to finish this book, no matter what it takes."

Me: (exaggerated disapproval) "Even if your sink is full of dishes?!"

Kathleen: (laughing) "Even if my sink is full of dishes, and the laundry isn't done, and my hair is greasy."

Me: "Those are all signs of a woman who is making her book more important than a sink full of dishes!"

Kathleen: "Oh I love that! The fact that my house is a mess is actually a confirmation that I am a success!"

(Don't tell the marketing team at Proctor and Gamble that we've figured this out!)

Gratitude as a Business Strategy

If we can start each day from a place of gratitude and abundance for what we already have, we have a much better chance of building a successful business. It's counterintuitive, but it really is critical.

This is of particular importance for coaches, because our potential and current clients can absolutely sense when we are in a state of calm contentment or nervous desperation. Have you ever had anyone try to sell you something and you just *knew* that they cared more about the sale than serving you? Fucking. Gross. When we are in a state of neediness, our clients will scatter like cockroaches when the lights come on.

Gratitude is the antidote to feeling jealous and not enough. When you feel good, you get to... feel good! Worth its weight in gold, I would say. Side bonus: You can more effectively enroll clients from this place. Your clients don't really care about the coaching model, or how many hours you have trained. They don't care if your business card has raised letters or if your website is connected to your social media strategy. They want to believe that they can actually feel good *right now, today!*

When you are connected to the place of your *own* contentment, clients will flock to you because you are a living and breathing model of what is possible for them.

Pay Attention to What You're Paying Attention To

What can we do, practically speaking, to build our gratitude muscle? How can we shift this constant low-grade (or sometimes extremely high-grade) anxiety of "I don't have enough and I am not enough?" Practically speaking, we practice.

We start by paying attention to what we're paying attention to. Do I feel anxious or content? Do I feel proud of who I am or do I feel like I'm not enough? Am I enjoying my current success or obsessing about the next level? Am I savoring the beauty of my surroundings or am I comparing my kitchen to the cover of Martha Stewart Living? If you are feeling anxious, you are not in a state of gratitude.

Take a moment right now to see where you might stand on the spectrum between anxiety and gratitude. Now take a deep breath of appreciation. Tap into the part of you that can see your life through a lens of what is working. Feel the air move effortlessly through your body. Now take another deep breath. Reflect on everything that has brought you to this point. The courage you have. The intelligence. The willingness. Notice the breath in your body. Your ability to read, and learn, and grow. You are miraculous!

Now look around. And I don't care if your sink is full of dishes and your rug has a red wine stain from four months ago. Look around and appreciate who you are and where you are. Go ahead and take a moment to appreciate your surroundings... I'll be right here when you get back!

(Told you)

What was that like? Right now I see snow falling outside my window – the snowflakes are so soft and playful. It's like I'm living in a snow globe. And the crackle and smell of my wood stove is giving me life right now! The warmth of it is filling my house – what a blessing to have a warm house on a cold spring day.

I'm not a famous author and Oprah's not calling me yet, but what a pleasure to spend time sharing what I know with you and to hold a prayer that this will bring you closer to what you want, need, and deserve.

It's like taking a deep, cool drink in the middle of the desert. My shoulders relax. The corners of my mouth turn up ever so slightly. I hear the chirping of birds outside my window. A deep breath. I have arrived at my success. Who knew?!

You can practice this, too. Turn your attention to what is easy to appreciate – particularly when you're in a delicious moment. Then it will become a default even when things are not so delicious.

This practice is about tuning into the part of you that knows every moment, every relationship, every word, and every interaction in your life is an ally for your greatest good. It's welcoming back that inner child who knows how to be present and be delighted at the simple wonders that are always around us.

Will you get pulled out of this delicious space? Of course! All day, a hundred times a day. (I still hold that my greatest spiritual challenge is being on hold when I'm calling someone for customer service.) So, you get pulled out of it, and then you notice, and then you return to gratitude, again and again.

With practice, we end up spending more time in gratitude and finding our own ways to reconnect throughout the day. Just like we would work out our body on the yoga mat or in the gym, we need to work the muscle of gratitude which is so often atrophied by the environment around us.

Let's Make it Real

Keep a gratitude journal for *at least* a week. I recommend... forever. Designate a journal (or find the back of an envelope and a crayon) and take 5–10 minutes every day writing down your gratitudes. It helps to use your senses and be specific – this will help raise your energy and create a more resonant experience in your mind, body, and spirit. For example, instead of "I'm appreciating my house," try "I'm appreciating the deep colors of the painting on the wall over my piano that I bought on our trip to Cape Cod."

Let the writing be sensual and pleasurable. Notice how it makes you feel. If it starts to feel like a burden, just let it go. You can also play this game with your mind and your attention.

With time, this will start to become a default so that even in trickier times, you'll be able to turn it on. Just yesterday, I was running late to a meeting because there was more traffic than usual. I could feel myself getting anxious and cranky, so I took a deep breath and noticed what I was paying attention to. I shifted my attention from lack to gratitude by taking a deep breath and cracking open the window. I turned off the radio and looked up at the gorgeous blue sky. I appreciated the sturdiness of my car in the snow.

I arrived seven minutes late to the meeting but – being in this space of gratitude – I didn't feel harried. The two women I was meeting were happily chatting when I arrived and we accomplished everything in the meeting that needed to be accomplished.

You have great power with this "attitude of gratitude" as some clever folks like to say. It is the antidote to jealousy; it is the remedy for racing the clock. Let it become your new normal to appreciate the world that surrounds you in every moment.

Other gratitude practices:

Start your coaching sessions with gratitude and notice what shifts. Ask your client to notice what they are grateful for in this moment or start with a sincere appreciation for who they are.

Bring gratitude to your family dinners: "What are you grateful for?" or "What was the very best part of your day today?" Model appreciation for your kids and colleagues and watch your world transform.

Start meetings with everyone offering an appreciation about the subject at hand. This primes the brain for creativity and innovation, by the way.

VISION

"When we open ourselves to desire, we open ourselves to being completely remade. A desire is the interface between you and that which is greater than you."

–REGENA THOMASHAUER, *PUSSY: A RECLAMATION*

I wish we taught the skill of visioning to young people. Scratch that! I wish young people taught adults how to hold onto the power of imagination and visioning. We are all born with the power to imagine and envision, but like many things outside of the realm of reason and logic, it is not a terribly valued skill in our culture.

As a coach – or any human really – vision is a critical component to creating the lives we deeply desire, and in serving our clients to do the same. All of us have dreams and desires. What I have discovered as a coach is that often when we open the box to our dreams and shine a flashlight on the interior, we find there's not much detail inside.

I'll never forget when my first coach, Bonnie Cohen, asked me in our first session, "What do you really want?" What a question! I responded with something like, "I don't really know. That's a good question. I guess I want to be a successful artist and I want to make more money."

"What would it look like if your wildest dream came true?"

Mind. Fucking. Blown.

I had never taken the time to really consider what it would actually look like! I had never considered that it was a possibility! We spent an hour luxuriating in the details of my vision. I imagined performing on stages around the world. I imagined coaching amazing people on a daily basis and making millions doing it. I imagined walking in the woods and making soup in my beautiful kitchen with a wood stove. We unpacked the box of my deepest desires and created an entire multi-dimensional life in technicolor.

Of course, that hour was delightful. I had lots of doubts and fears and excuses popping up but she just danced around them with questions like, "Who's going to be at your first CD release show? How are you going to spend twenty thousand dollars a month?" and the big whammy, "Who do you need to BE to make this vision a reality?"

As I stumbled my way forward, I found myself performing and writing more. Some shows, I made a profit and some shows, I lost money. I worked with more clients and started to charge more. Some were my dream clients and some were just not a fit. But as I stayed tethered to the vision, I stayed tethered to the woman I was becoming, because *that vision was in my bones* and it pulled me through all of it.

A big and clear vision compels us to make decisions from the person we are becoming rather than the person we are today. This is when change begins to happen.

Vision as a Business Strategy

I had an amazing client named Donald: mid-40s father with a gorgeous wife and two daughters. He had been working in a corporate job that didn't fit his talents, and he couldn't stand it anymore. He knew that he wanted to be a coach, but he felt like he had no idea how to get started, and he was feeling uninspired.

I started with vision by asking some simple but powerful questions: "What do you want?" "Who do you want to work with?" "What kind of income would support your vision?" He was answering the questions but the energy was flat. I asked him, "What do you *really* want?"

"I know this is crazy but I think I want to live in Maine!" he said immediately. "My wife and I have always wanted to move there but it's just not realistic. My family is all down here and my mother really needs me around..."

Just like Bonnie who had so sweetly danced around *my* excuses, I asked, "What else would you create from your house in Maine?"

"Oh man!! I would walk on the beach and have lobster bakes! I keep seeing an image of a tree and a swing. I would write and coach and start my own men's group...."

As we continued to explore his desire and his vision, the details poured in as his map of intention became clearer and clearer. "Who do you need to be to make this vision real?" I asked. "I need to be brave. I need to be a leader in my family...."

This vision became an anchor for all of our future coaching. With every topic he brought to the table, that image of the house in Maine was like smelling salts when he would pass out in a trance of excuses or apathy.

When the vision is clear and resonant, it has the power to call you forth through the journey of making it real.

Donald lives two blocks away from me now. In Maine. With a backyard. Near the beach. He was walking his dog last week while we were burning our Christmas tree in the backyard. We had a giant hug. It made me very happy.

Inviting Income into Your Big Vision

Your big vision will not be realized unless the finances are there to support it. In every coaching course I've ever led, there are always questions around money and coaching, and what I've noticed over the years is that most of the questions come from a place of profound anxiety and scarcity:

"Should I charge at all as a new coach?"

"I'm thinking of doing sessions for free because I'm still learning these skills."

"I don't want to limit myself, so I think I'll charge $25 so that my clients have access to this work."

Money stirs up a lot of thoughts, beliefs, and emotions, and for many of us, they are not generally abundant or life-affirming. For many new coaches, selling a service is an entirely new and often confronting experience. But here's the deal:

If you want to build a coaching business that supports your life financially, you are going to have to charge more than $25 a session. Think about it. You are trading hours for money as a coach, so even if you were *very* successful at finding committed clients at $25 a session (you won't) and managed to see seven clients a day (that's rough and also you'll need time for marketing so let's say seven clients a day, three days a week), that's $175 a day, $525 a week, and about $27k a year.

Oh... then self-employment tax. And then you get sick. And then you start losing clients because they're not committed. So you're looking at 20k a year. Is that doable for you? What kind of life does that give you? How would you show up to your clients? What would you do when your clients come to you saying that more than anything, they want financial freedom?

If You Can't Support Yourself, You Can't Support Others

What I've seen – more times than I can bear – is talented and brilliant coaches who don't charge enough money to make a living, so they end up resigning themselves to a stable job that they hate. This is not the vision! If you don't find a way to support yourself financially through your coaching, you will be serving fewer people, and your mission will die. Your future clients also pay a price because they never get to *work with you*. When I realized this in my own journey, it almost felt selfish not to do the work to get to a place of confident pricing and joyful receiving of the financial cream.

We need to be honest about how much financial fluid we must open ourselves to receiving in order to keep our mission alive and well.

Stand in Your Value as a Coach

For years, I have heard new coaches ask some version of the question, "How can I charge $200, $400, $800 just to sit and listen to someone?!" First of all this is a *hugely* valuable commodity in our busy world today. How often do we sit and listen deeply and without distraction to another person in our busy lives? My executive clients say that our sessions are the best part of their week and it's because they finally have a chance to sit still, reflect, and be listened to deeply.

Furthermore, you are not just sitting and listening. You are using all of your incredible skill and insight to support your client in solving a problem that really matters to them. To be crystal clear, I am not saying that your client is a problem to be fixed. I'm saying that your client will *hire* you because they believe you have a solution to their problem.

I train all of my coaches in how to make "sales calls" with total integrity and ease because they understand how to listen for the client's pain and assess if they can support them in solving it. When it's a match, the coach is able to confidently sell their coaching and feel great about it. The client is able to sign up for the coaching and feel great about it. There is no sleaze and there is no manipulation. Just lots of clients getting results and lots of coaches making a living doing what they love.

People spend money to solve problems and as a coach, you are well equipped to serve people in facing those problems and moving toward their dream come true.

You are valuable. Coaching is valuable. Just because it's fun and fulfilling and relatively easy for you doesn't mean it's not valuable.

Putting a Pricetag on Coaching

Charge what the solution is worth to your client, not the price that you're comfortable with.

How much is it worth for your client to have their dreams come true? If you can't answer that question easily, then I want you to consider a real challenge you have right now? Do you want to quit your dead-end job? Find the partner of your dreams? Find a way to work and travel at the same time? Get into the best physical shape of your life? Ask yourself how much would it be worth for you to solve this problem for good? I know for sure it's more than $25.

Let's do this, warrior. Let's get this money situation cleaned up and cleared out and ready to flow – so that you can live your purpose, give more and receive more, and model it to others so that they can do the same.

Money Consciousness as a Business Strategy

Your inner relationship to all things money is what affects your outer financial results, and we are building this business from the inside out. Here are some activities and habits that will help to shift your inner relationship toward financial abundance.

If this feels scary, consider my friend Kate Northrup's words, "I know when I started to get really honest with myself about my money, it was painful. But it wasn't as painful as staying stuck in financial unconsciousness with a nagging feeling that I was living without integrity." Give yourself and your future clients the gift of facing your financial world.

1.   Look at your numbers every single day.

If someone asked me 13 years ago how much money I had in my checking account, I wouldn't have had a clue. I wouldn't *want* to look. I didn't know if there was $300 or an overdraft of $300. These days you can ask me on any given day how much money I have in my checking, business, and savings accounts, and I can tell you within $5 or so. Why? Because I take 45 seconds to look at my bank accounts at least once a day.

When you don't know what you have, this makes spending money extremely stressful! "Can I afford these groceries?

Can I afford to go to dinner with my girlfriends? Can I afford those Nine West turquoise flats that make my heart sing? I don't know, so... I guess I'll do it anyway and then stress out about it. Or I won't do it and then I'll feel terribly resentful about it." Turning around to face the monster and look it in the eye and talk to it and make a plan with it is always less painful than ignoring it as it looms larger and larger behind your back.

2.   Whatever numbers are there – be thankful.

If you have $25, be thankful. If you have $2, be thankful. If you have over drafted, feel proud that you are facing it. No matter what, be thankful that you have an income. (See Chapter One.)

3.   Clear out your junk drawer.

And your underwear drawer and your garage and your closet. Release things that do not give you a sense of abundance and joy. Make space for receiving abundant income. Make space for your wealth.

4.   Pay your bills right away and pay them with gratitude.

Almost everyone complains about bills... it's what people do! But real talk: Do we like having running water? What about electricity? Heat in the house? A running car? Beautiful clothing? If we love the things that our bills represent, why are we so bitter about paying for them?

When I stopped being resentful about my bills, and started being grateful (I literally still write "thank you!" in the memo of all of my checks – try it!) it not only shifted my experience of bill paying, it also helped me be more discerning about what I was spending money on. Does this product or service truly bring me joy or solve an important problem? If it doesn't, then I don't buy it.

5. **Don't make assumptions about what people will invest in.**

When we have our own shit about money, we project it all over the place, including on our beloved clients. Just because we tell ourselves we can't afford something doesn't mean that they can't.

When I worked in a high-end salon, I trained everyone to offer the same product recommendations to everyone, regardless of what they looked like or what assumptions we were making about them. Very often the person we assumed *couldn't* afford it would spend all kinds of cash on hairspray and lipstick, and the person who looked like a million bucks would say "no thanks" and leave a shitty tip.

Your job is not to assume what people are willing to spend. Your job is to stand in your value as a coach.

Let's Make it Real

Now that you understand the role that money plays in your big vision, what is *your Big Vision goal*? How will you know you've arrived at it? It's so important to have a specific and outrageous dream that will pull you forward rather than shut you down. Your vision is a map for where you're going next *and* a thrilling final destination that will call you forth when things get hard.

The purpose of the vision is to keep you moving forward with excitement and clarity; it is *not necessarily* a prediction of what will happen in your life. Only God knows where we will end up if we keep listening and responding to divine guidance!

What's your big vision goal in the next 10–15 years? You should be able to say "yes" or "no" when you ask the question "Have I accomplished this goal?" In other words, make it specific and measurable (and totally, outrageously thrilling). "I'm a guest on Oprah's Super Soul Sunday," is a specific – and probably thrilling – goal. "I'm working with lots of clients" is not.

After you have identified your long-term big vision goal, identify the shorter-term goal in the next 12–18 months. Again, this should be specific and measurable, but let's not worry about realistic for now.

Now think about who you are being at each of these milestones. What did it take for you to get there? What are the qualities of that human? How is she being? How is she *not* being? What is she wearing? How does she spend her mornings? What does she eat for lunch?

I take all of my clients through a guided visualization to energetically meet this "Future Self" on a deep level. I have done this with hundreds of clients and it never ceases to amaze me the detail and wisdom that comes through. You can contact me **megan@meganjowilson.com** and I will send you a recorded version of this visualization, or you can do some journaling to hear from your Future Self (try writing from her voice with your non-dominant hand!). Of course I also recommend bringing this topic to your own coach for a deeper understanding. This Future Self is a powerful inner resource for moving toward your wildly successful coaching business.

A vision board is another fun and powerful tool to deepen your clarity and commitment to either of these goals, if that appeals to you. We engage our creative selves by cutting and pasting images and words to a board that we can refer to as we stumble forward. Typically, after I make a vision board (and I could open a small gallery since this is one of my favorite ways to get clearer), it's not as much the aftermath as the doing itself. The process should keep you in a state of energetic resonance and excitement. If it feels like a chore, skip it.

I'm old school in that I recommend getting actual magazines, scissors, and glue sticks. It takes longer than clicking images on Pinterest, and as a result, it engages our emotional, mental, and spiritual energies more intensely and for a longer period. This process sets all kinds of magical things in motion.

Ultimately, I want you to be able to answer each of the questions below and to hold them deep in your mind, body, and soul (you could write your answers on the back of the vision board):

What is the big vision goal for your coaching business in the next 10–15 years?

_____

_____

What is your big vision goal for your coaching business in the next 12–18 months?

_____

_____

Who are your ideal clients?

_____

_____

Who are you being?

_____

_____

What's the impact you're having on your clients and on your world?

_____

_____

How much financial fluid is flowing into your life each month (long term and short term and be specific!)?

_____

_____

Where are you investing your time, energy, and money?

_____

_____

What are you most proud of?

_____

_____

The outcome and vision should be incredibly specific and compelling. When it is, you will be able to put all of your actions and decisions through the filter, "Does this align with my vision and my outcomes?" You will always hear a clear "yes" and a clear "no" when your vision is specific and thrilling. I recommend that you respond to those answers accordingly!

SERVICE

"I never joined big networking events or paid a lot for a fancy web page. I chose to invest in creating real value for each and every client. I don't need a manual to connect with a human being and serve them. When you find value for yourself, you will become unstoppable."

–L.A. REDING, MCC

When we don't know who we're serving, we are lost. We cannot find our clients, and our clients certainly cannot find us, and therefore we are not coaching and we are not making the difference we were born to make. Do you know who you are serving? I am talking about your ideal client.

What is an "ideal client?" First of all, your ideal client wants to work with *you*. You, who will be their very most favorite coach in the whole world, for everything that you are and with all of your quirks, and beliefs, and your style, and your approach. Your ideal client inspires you and loves to absorb all of the goodness you have to offer. But this ideal client will never find you until you claim who you are and who you are called to serve.

"I don't want to limit myself," is the most common refrain of resistance I hear when it comes to defining the ideal client. I get it. If you are a creative visionary, you don't want to feel like you're being pinned down or limited in any way, shape, or form. But I promise you it's one of the most freeing things you can do for yourself and for the success of your business.

When we clarify our ideal clients, and eventually our niche, a phenomenal thing happens. We become *extremely* visible to others. I believe that this vulnerable experience of becoming exposed and visible is at the heart of why so many new coaches resist it.

Defining Your Ideal Client

Here is the critical piece you need to understand: Defining your ideal client does *not* mean that you will only and actually be *working with* that kind of person. You will end up working with all *kinds* of people who don't look exactly like your ideal client, except in the sense that they are dying to hire you.

These people will come to you saying things like, "I know you typically work with women, but I'm a man and I have that same problem – would you work with me?" Or, "I saw what you did with my wife and she said it was all about accountability. Can you do that for me and my business?" In other words, the possibilities become limitless. Here's the deal:

The more specifically you define your ideal client, the more clients you will serve.

Did you really hear that?

The more narrow and specific your ideal client, the more clients you will enroll and work with.

Let's Test It

When I tell you I'm a life coach (which is true) do you think of *specific* people in your real life that you could refer to me? Probably not so much.

When I tell you I'm a life coach that works with other coaches, do you actually think of specific people you know in your real circle of connections that you would refer to me? (I doubt it because you probably know lots of other coaches).

When I tell you I'm a life coach that works with coaches who want to start a coaching business, do you think of specific people you know? (Maybe, but then again many coaches want to start a business.)

When I tell you I'm a life coach that works with new coaches who are spiritually-oriented women in their 40s who are ready to step into their true power and build a fulfilling and profitable coaching business, and have a damn good time doing it... do you think of specific names of actual women that you know, who you would refer to me?

I really want you to check that out. Do specific people start to come to mind now that I've gotten that specific? What if I said "I work with stay-at-home-moms"? Or, "stay-at-home moms who used to work in corporate?" Or, "stay at home moms over 40 years old who used to work in corporate and want to lose 15 pounds and feel sexy again."

Do you see how the more specific I get, the easier it is for you to think of actual people? Suddenly my name became clearer in your head and you made a connection between me and all of the fabulous stay-at-home mammas who are ready to feel sexy again. (I'm kind of loving this ideal client. I think it's a great niche!)

If that were my actual ideal client, here's what would happen next: You would think of me if you heard a man complaining about losing 15 pounds, and you might even refer them to me. You would think of me if you talked to a stay-at-home mom who doesn't need to lose weight, but who could really use a life coach because she's going through a divorce.

Now that you can *see* me in the crowd of a million other coaches, you will start making connections to me and my coaching business.

Being Seen is Being Vulnerable

Knowing your ideal client allows you to be seen. It forces you to be seen, in fact, and I think that's why so many coaches subconsciously resist it. We say that it's because we don't want to limit ourselves, but what we're really feeling is, "I'm not ready to be seen as an expert yet." "What if I can't deliver?" "Will this audience resonate with me?" "What if I look stupid or my marketing materials aren't strong enough?"

I get all of those doubts and fears because I have faced them myself and I'm certainly facing them while I write this book:

This book makes no sense.

Who am I to think I can write a book?

Is anyone going to benefit from this?

My brilliant colleagues are going to tear this apart.

And do you know what gets me back on track?

My ideal client.

Because I care more about serving my ideal client than I do serving my doubts and fears. I *know* that my ideal client was born to have a thriving coaching business, and I would do *anything* to get her out in the world, and living her purpose, and touching lives – being a part of an army of light that this world so desperately wants and needs.

That's the really great thing about this. Knowing your ideal client will actually help you get over yourself and get into action. You are a warrior, after all, who has been called to serve.

Define your ideal client so that she can find you. If it feels vulnerable or exposing to be seen in such a new and powerful way, remember that people are way more concerned about themselves than they are about picking you apart.

Service as a Business Strategy

Confession: When I started coaching, I resisted this ideal client thing with all of my being. "How can I pick *one person* of the population?! How would I even know where to begin?! There are so many options and what if I change my mind?!" So I didn't commit. I marketed myself as a "life coach" for about 8 years and I worked with anyone. I attracted a lot of artists because I was a musician, and a bunch of women because I was a woman, and I attracted a lot of basically unemployed people because I was broke.

Your clients will always show up the way you do.

I was desperate for clients. I did the most ridiculous incentive programs you could think of. None of them worked. Word of mouth would get me a new client from time to time, but asking my clients to articulate to their friends what I was offering was tricky. How could I expect them to do it when I couldn't even do it for myself?!

Look at any successful coach and you will see that they know exactly who they are serving. My client Amy Young is an amazing success story and a total model for the power of service. Just like you, Amy can coach anyone. She can coach any person about any topic because she's a fabulous fucking coach. But her business is built around one specific client: a young woman who is stressed out and confused about dating, romance, and relationships.

She has a YouTube channel that just hit over 62 thousand views and certainly more by your reading of this book. She has endless streams of high-paying clients. If you are stressed out and confused about dating, romance, and relationships, you will probably go to her YouTube channel soon. You really should. She's terribly wise and also hilarious.

If you don't check her out, you are at least thinking of a handful of your friends who could use her... I know I am! I send clients to her *all the time* – even though I *myself* could coach them because I automatically make that connection in my mind.

Another of my warrior clients in The Army of Light is Talia Guten who works with women in their first-quarter who are interested in yoga, meditation, and spirituality. Now, every time I meet a woman in her early 20s who seems to be interested in health and wellness, I send them to Talia. I also send women in their 20s who are not interested in health and wellness, as well as women in their 50s who love yoga.

These two warriors are so connected and committed to serving their clients that they are willing to stand out and be seen and to make mistakes and to keep going. Yes, they are experiencing more financial freedom than they probably ever have, but they are also experiencing the *fulfillment* of making a difference. They are doing the work they were born to do.

Let's Make it Real

Who is the person you feel called to serve? Do you know her name? Where she lives? What keeps her up at night? What her greatest fear is? What about her dream come true?

If you are struggling to define your ideal client, one place to look is into your past. Check out the you that you were before you got to where you are now. This younger version of you has a problem or a challenge that you know very well and you are probably very well suited to help her solve it because you solved it (or at least a portion of it which is useful for your ideal client).

Now I want you to go make a cup of something yummy and sit down with a pen and paper – or your computer – for half an hour or so to write a *detailed* bio of your ideal client. Even if you're not quite sure yet, write it as if you are researching a character for your novel or for a movie. The director (you) needs to know every detail about this character. Answer these questions:

What's your ideal client's full name?

How old is she?

Dating, married, single? For how long?

What is she doing for income?

For fun? What is she Googling? What is she obsessing about right now? What is causing her pain?

What is her dream come true? The dream that feels so far-fetched it could not possibly ever happen even though a tiny part of her thinks that maybe it could happen somehow?

What is she currently doing to move closer to that dream? What does she wear? Where does her family live?

Does she have siblings?

What music does she listen to? Who are her best friends and what do they do when they get together?

Who does she turn to for help?

What problem would she pay *any* amount to have solved?

Bonus: Create a vision board of your ideal client OR create the vision board you know that *she* would create! Find images or photos that capture her essence. Make a playlist of the music she is listening to. Find creative ways to know this person as intimately as you can so that you two can find each other!

She is out there and she is *dying* to hire you. Make that easy for her!

INSPIRATION

"Make every breath count."

—ART SHIRK, LEADERSHIP COACH

In many ways, we are in the business of inspiration. So when I say to my clients who are coaches, "Enjoy your life like enjoyment is your job," I really mean it. I want you to treat your own sense of joy and fulfillment and delight as a top priority in running your business as a coach.

It is very difficult to sell your coaching when you feel like shit. I know it because I've tried. When I was charging $20 per session, and working with people I did not believe in, I was out of integrity with myself, my vision, and my purpose. Not so inspired. And because integrity matters so much to us as coaches, it's incredibly painful to stand in front of a client and say, *"You* can be successful.... *You* can have the life of your dreams.... *You* can make a living doing what you love," when we don't believe that we're doing that for ourselves.

This is the best and the most challenging part of being a coach: We have to (get to!) walk the line of really working toward our own sense of inspiration with total conviction, while at the same time accepting that we are human and imperfect, and appreciating where we are *right now*. Allow yourself to make mistakes, and be committed to learning from them. Be committed to moving toward fulfillment and returning to that path over and over again when you get off track.

In all my career as a coach, I have never had a client who came to me because of my credentials. Every client I've worked with came to me because they were inspired by my passion for the things I do and love, and my willingness to take bold action in the name of my purpose.

My life is beautiful. It is also a mess. And I'm not embarrassed to admit that. I don't want to work with clients who expect me to be some guru who claims to be enlightened. I want to work with clients who are inspired by the way I have committed myself to moving in that direction with everything I've got, and who are interested in doing the same.

I make mistakes. I get depressed. I lose connection sometimes with who I really am and what really matters to me. But ever since I met coaching, and had a taste of the power of delight and pleasure, I've been seeking it out like a pig sniffing for truffles. I've put a lot of time and energy into asking myself "What do I really want?" and then moving in that direction with all of the focus and tenacity I can possibly muster. This is your most important job.

"What do I really want?" can change from day to day or season to season, but to build a thriving coaching practice, you must answer this question over and over, and you must move in that direction. Your clients will smell your commitment from miles away, and they will smell the lack of it as well.

If this is feeling like a lot of pressure, or a burden that you're not sure you can live up to, take a deep breath and consider viewing it as the very best part of being a warrior coach. You *get* to have a job that requires you to walk your talk, where the "talk" is something like, "We can choose to live a life on purpose. We can choose to appreciate and maybe even enjoy this vicious, brilliant, brutal, miraculous life." So how *do we* make that choice?

When You're Inspired, You Are Inspiring

One assignment I give to my clients who are building a coaching business, is to get very good at noticing the things that are inspiring or the things that "give them life." I ask them to be like researchers on a mission to discover what kinds of activities, relationships, beliefs, and objects give a sense of pleasure, delight, and energy, and what of those things do not.

I've become so completely accustomed to this practice that – for better or worse – I find that I have a very low tolerance for life-diminishing activities. Although it's not always easy, I have learned to turn away from jobs, relationships, and conversations that drain my energy. I walk out of restaurants if the host is an asshole. I change direction if my work doesn't inspire me. I find a new way to work out if I start to get bored. I leave relationships that are life-diminishing. This has gotten easier with practice.

One of my most beloved mentors is a brilliant coach and coach trainer named Art Shirk. "Make every breath count," was his message to the world before he passed away last year from a terminal lung disease. "Make every breath count," is the same message I hear from my first coach Bonnie Cohen who died of cancer, and I hear it again in the spirit of my mentor Elaine Jaynes who was also taken away from the earthly realm by that same disease. What is the best way for us to honor the lives of the people we love? We can make every breath count and we can help our clients do the same.

If it Doesn't Inspire You, Shut it Down

Yes, I know you have people in your lives that you can't get rid of, and you have responsibilities that matter. But I'm officially giving you permission to avoid the things that do not inspire you whenever possible, even and especially when you think they might be good for you.

There are hundreds of fellow entrepreneur coaches who are teaching about online funnels that will generate thousands of clients in a matter of months. I signed up for a couple of their programs out of curiosity and I have to admit that it turned me off. Their lines were scripted and their energy felt fake to me. So I stopped signing up.

Could that information be useful for me and my business?

Absolutely. Could I force myself to sit through it? Yep. And many of my colleagues would say that doing so is the most important part of my work. I disagree. I say the most important part of our work as coaches and humans is to feel inspired and to do whatever we can to build more esteem for ourselves, not less.

Choosing Inspiration

I remember grappling one afternoon with where I "should" be putting my energy. As always, I had some paperwork and emailing to do for my business, but I was really craving some alone time in the kitchen. I had the ingredients to make some homemade soup – one of my top 100 life-giving activities – so I stepped away from my computer and started prepping my vegetables.

The computer was open on the kitchen table as I tried to cut the vegetables as fast as I could. Then as the onions were sizzling, I'd go to my email and start a response with greasy fingers. (Yay multi-tasking! Modern America's obsession and, in my opinion, probably one the most damaging of all aspirations on earth!)

When I caught myself in this torturous cycle, I made one simple decision that changed the course of my life. I chose to close the computer and chose to make the soup. As if that wasn't life-changing enough (and it really is sometimes a radical act to close the computer), I decided to take my time making the soup. I would not frantically cut the vegetables; I would enjoy the sharpness of the knife and the biting scent of green peppers. I would carefully wipe down the counters and taste the broth as I went. I chose to return to the deliciousness of what was happening in front of me.

I understood in this mundane moment that as a coach, it was my *job* and my *responsibility* to enjoy making the soup. If I couldn't model this for myself and my family, how could I take a stand for it for others?! Suddenly, making this soup became a critical part of running my business. It became the *most* important part of running my business. And if this was true of soup-making, it must also be true for woods-walking, and love-making, and beach-napping, and wine-drinking.

Yes – we have to send emails and do paperwork and show up for coaching calls and write the damn book, but *how* I do those things is more important than just doing them. Can I show up to my emails with a sense of focus? Can I pay my bills with presence and gratitude? Will I allow myself to *choose* to stay in bed and stare into my true love's eyes... with nowhere to go and nothing to prove? This is the *best* part of being a coach because we will fall off the wagon again and again and again. But it is our responsibility to get back on track by choosing our life instead of having it happen to us.

Inspired Taxes (No, That is Not a Typo!)

My client Jan was a brilliant coach who – like most of my clients – was passionate about the work of coaching but really felt lost when it came to managing her money. She had a long history of debt and tons of shame about how she had been leaning into financial support from her family. "I should know how to manage my money," was a demon that kept her awake at night, even though managing her money had never been taught or modeled to her.

Tax time came and Jan was in true despair. The overwhelm was almost unbearable. She would bring the topic to our coaching and then would break down in tears at the thought of getting started. This brilliant, creative woman was giving all of her power away when it came to facing the responsibilities of managing money. There was no joy and pleasure for Jan so there was no energy. We started by exploring some of the many limiting beliefs she had about money, as well as some of the fabulous reasons she had for clinging to those beliefs and then I asked, "How can doing your taxes be the most pleasurable part of your day?"

She laughed.

So I asked again. "How can doing your taxes be a pleasure?"

"I don't know... maybe I should just put on some music and dance around the room first!"

"What kind of music would support you in facing your taxes?"

She was a little taken aback that I was considering her crazy idea. But it didn't take long for her to respond with crystal clarity, "Yo-Yo Ma!"

"What else would make it a pleasure?"

"A really good cup of herbal tea with lemon."

"Nice... what do you love about herbal tea with lemon?"

"I love that it's fresh and yellow and refreshing. It sort of cuts through the yuck." (Jan is an artist and a sensual woman... can you tell?)

"Yellow and refreshing. You could choose to do your taxes in a yellow, refreshing way with good tea and cello concertos."

We are so powerful when we choose how to see something and experience something. It takes some practice (and often some coaching) but it *is* possible.

Inspired Exercise (Also Not a Typo!)

My client Mona was eating some pretzels when she first walked into my office in baggy jeans and a loose sweater. We chatted for a while and then I asked her, "What's the biggest change you would like to see in your life in the next three months?"

"I would like to lose weight," she said without skipping a beat. "I've been saying that since 5th grade but honestly, if I could change anything, I would lose weight."

I started asking some more questions about why this mattered to her and eventually we started circling around her relationship to exercise. I will never forget the way she pounded her fist into her open palm as she leaned forward in her chair.

"You don't understand. I *hate* exercise."

I became curious about her hatred of exercise and noticed that everything she hated about it had to do with her associations of pain and suffering. This woman was a graphic designer who loved beauty and luxury. Like every other woman I've ever met on the planet Earth, she was a *pleasure junkie*! She just didn't know it. She hated exercise because there was no pleasure in it.

She wasn't quite sure if she believed my theory, but she was willing to experiment. She spent 30 more dollars for a membership at a gym that was clean, and exclusive, and had a great locker room with lavender soap. She came back the following week and said she loved it. She signed a year contract. She kept working out and found new strength in her body and that inspired her to do more. With Goddess as my witness, this woman is now a personal trainer and her body is slammin' rock-hard, gorgeous. This woman who said, "You don't understand. I hate exercise," had turned her life around through the power of pleasure. Do not underestimate the power of pleasure and fulfillment in your journey.

Inspiration as a Business Strategy

When *you* live as an inspired coach, you can hold that space for your clients and ask, "What would be possible if you stopped settling? What would happen if you chose pleasure and inspiration every single day, even when you're working on your business? What if you made fulfillment your top priority?"

This reframe about inspiration means that pleasure and enjoyment become a *part of* your responsibility as a professional coach. It means that you get to live on purpose and *choose* how to spend your time, rather than slumping into it unconsciously.

There are two ways to watch Netflix (or eat a meal, or take a nap, or lift weights, or talk with a friend or any activity on earth):

You *choose* to watch it on purpose and with full permission.

You find yourself just sort of watching it because it's in front of you, and now you're not even enjoying it because you really feel like you should be doing something else with your time and there is this low buzz of guilt sitting next to you the whole time.

Watch your Netflix on purpose, coach.

Go to the gym – or not – on purpose, coach.

Build your business – or not – on purpose, coach.

The way to know if you have made a conscious choice about what you're doing, is to notice the energy of it and the way you feel about it. You will feel peaceful, clear, settled, and aligned when you *choose* to take a nap. You will feel like you're cuddling up with your guilt when you don't.

Let's Make it Real

Be a researcher of your own inspiration. Notice what gives you life and energy and notice what drains it. Keep a journal this week and capture what you notice.

Start a list of 100 life-giving activities and make them specific. For example, "making home-made soup" vs. "cooking." Write down as many as you can *right now*.

Here's the part that really matters, dear warrior: Choose two that you will do *today*. No more waiting on feeling good.

Choose to feel good. Choose to be inspired. Feel good like it's your job.

Because it is.

CONFIDENCE

"If you want to enroll clients, you have to believe that coaching is the best thing that could happen to someone."

–HENRY KIMSEY-HOUSE, CO-FOUNDER OF CTI

My client Raquel had a clear sense of her purpose as a life coach. She knew without a doubt that this was her life's calling. But she wasn't moving forward with the things she knew she had to do to get paying clients and she couldn't figure out why. She was editing her bio every week, building and re-building her website, and researching networking events in her town. When she met new people she would introduce herself as a "coach-in-training who is also waiting tables at Rosita's Pub to pay the bills." Then she would change the subject.

Raquel was being run by a powerful limiting belief which was "I'm too young. People won't take me seriously." She believed that other people wouldn't take her seriously because *she* wasn't taking herself seriously. And although Raquel was indeed in her early twenties, this refrain of doubt is one I have heard from new coaches of all ages:

"I'm not ready yet." "I need more training and practice."

"Once I finish my classes (get certified, finish my website, design my business cards...), then I will start to look for clients in earnest."

"Who the *fuck* am I to be a coach?!"

For Raquel, and for many new coaches, it makes perfect sense that the primary obstacle is a lack of confidence, which is born out of a belief that the confidence will come "as soon as I have more experience... as soon as I finish my certification... as soon as I have a real office with a printer... as soon as I lose 10 pounds..." (fill in your own blank).

Earn Your Confidence

Carolyn Myss says, "Earn your confidence," and I love this bold statement. It implies that we shouldn't be confident yet if we're starting something new, so I don't have to "fake it till you make it." I don't want to fake anything! I want to be real about where I'm at. So if I'm not confident yet, so what? I will get there by doing. By practicing. By stumbling forward imperfectly, or gloriously.

The big secret is that there is no way to get good at something without first being inept. It's a stage of learning called "conscious incompetence" which is a fancy way of saying, "I know enough to know how much I don't know." It's very uncomfortable for our ego that totally thrives on looking good.

So what does this mean for you as a new coach? I'm encouraging you to go out and practice with clients but you don't really have the confidence. You get it on paper, but it sounds kind of nerve-wracking. Well, go do it anyway, warrior! Connect yourself to your soul purpose and move forward imperfectly. Why? Because you have so very much to offer to your clients *right now*. Who the fuck are you NOT to be a coach?

When we release perfection ("I need to be a master coach in order to launch a successful business."), we can get excited again about bringing all of the incredibly useful tools, attitudes, and skills we already have to our wonderful clients. This can be a huge boost in confidence for new coaches.

You are wise, warrior. You have been through some things in life that brought you to coaching. You are not here because you want a mediocre life. You are here because you know that you are called to have a life of meaning, and a life that touches others. I'm telling you that the best way to do this is to dare to know it, trust it, and share it. Not so that you can prove that you're a guru, but so that your clients can find you and benefit from all the gifts that you have to offer.

Dare to be seen. Dare to shine. Make it easy for your clients to find you. You don't need to be an expert at 20 things. Be an expert at *one* thing that you love. Just one. Just pick one thing you and then keep moving in that direction with everything you've got. For years, I coached anyone who was willing to show up, and I found myself getting bored.

After doing some inner research, I discovered that all I ever really wanted to talk about was coaching and spirituality. So I started working with coaches who were spiritually-oriented and suddenly I couldn't wait for Monday morning to arrive. This is what we're going for.

Confidence as a Business Strategy

What can you guarantee to your clients? (I'll get you started):

I can listen deeply to them.

I can help them notice their limiting beliefs.

I can encourage them authentically.

I can help them articulate their values and dreams.

I can create a safe space for them to feel their joy and pain.

Now add a few of your own. Please, for the love of your clients... add a few (or a few hundred) of your own!

Can you see how valuable this is? You must be willing to share this with the world and with your potential clients.

Now let's take it to the next level: What outcomes will your clients enjoy? I'll start you off with a few, based on the points above.

As a result of working with me as your coach:

You will learn to listen to yourself more deeply.

You will notice your own limiting beliefs.

You will be able to move around your limiting beliefs so that you can move toward the life you really want.

You will feel encouraged which will build your own sense of self-esteem so that you can move toward the life you really want.

You will be able to articulate your values and your dreams which will help you move toward the life you really want starting *now*.

Write down some of your own. What will your clients get as a result of working with you? What unique life experience and knowledge can you bring to your coaching?

What Do You Believe?

The next thing I ask new coaches to do is articulate their beliefs. Not beliefs like, "I believe Triscuits are better than Wheat Thins," (although I love this question).

What are your beliefs about life?

What has life taught you?

What do you hold to be true?

Whenever I offer this process, I can hear the chains falling off of a new coach who has been told that they are not meant to give advice or hold agendas for their clients. The beliefs pour out of them in gorgeous and clear statements that radiate total confidence. Here are some examples of real beliefs my clients have shared with me:

"The greatest lessons in life come out of our hardships."

"Everything that happens in our lives is for our highest good."

"We are always being taught an important lesson."

"We must put our own self-care at the top of the list if we want to care for others."

It can be an incredible confidence booster to see that you have value to offer, outcomes you can guarantee, and a strong sense of knowing from your own journey.

Here's one last crazy notion. What if confidence is a decision that you can make right now without any further external validation? What if you can actually decide to be confident even in the face of your doubts and fears and imperfections? Again, this is not "fake it till you make it." I don't want you to fake it. I want you to *decide* that you are confident for real. I dare you. This is what separates successful coaches from unsuccessful ones.

Let's Make it Real

Find a photo of yourself and make a visual that includes your face and some words that reflect the light of who you are: "Brilliant," "Courageous," and "Loving" are some good options (Word Swag is a fun app for this!) If you're ready to claim this truth about yourself for real in a safe tribe, post your photo in my Facebook Group, "Megan Jo Wilson & The Army of Light."

COMMITMENT

"Never. Fucking. Give up."

–ERIC KOHNER, LEADERSHIP COACH

Are you all in on building a successful coaching business? Or do you have a plan B? This is not to make you wrong if you do, but to notice the impact that it is having on your thoughts, your actions, and your results.

Take my client Ramona. She was just starting her business and doing her best to get clients for certification, and she had had a rough week. She had a couple of potential client rejections that she took pretty personally (I mean... that's a rough one, right?), and she was really starting to have doubts about her ability to make her coaching business real.

As we started to explore her doubts, I heard her say, "I know I'm meant to be a coach, I just don't know *how*."

"Bullshit," I said.

"What?!"

"If you *knew* beyond any shadow of a doubt that you were meant to be a coach, you wouldn't be doubting yourself right now," I replied. "You wouldn't be worried about the how, you would just start doing and learning and trying and trusting."

"But I don't *even have* clients right now! I had two chances last week and I blew it!"

"Yep. I get it. That's what learning feels like sometimes and that's when it's time to dig deep. Let's play a little game. Right now you're feeling shitty because you're doubting that you're meant to be a coach and doubting your ability to succeed. Your thought is, 'I *might* succeed as a coach... and I might not.'"

"Oh *God*, you're right!"

"Okay," I said. "So, as you stand in 'I might succeed but I'm not sure,' what's that like?"

"Ugh! I feel so depressed. I feel out of alignment with my future self. I feel totally overwhelmed about what I have to do and it makes me want to... go back to bed for the rest of the day."

Me: "Now, how about I tell you to go enroll some clients to live their dream from this place?!"

Ramona: "No way! How could I tell them to feel successful when I'm not feeling that way?! Ew I'm a fraud!!"

"No sweetheart, you're not a fraud," I reminded her. "You're a human being on a very courageous journey and you're noticing that you're stuck in a story that doesn't serve you.... So now I want you to imagine that I have a crystal ball. I can see all of time past, present, and future, and I am telling you, Ramona, you *are* meant to be a coach. I can see the future and you *are* going to succeed as a coach. It is written in the stars."

I waited a breath or two and asked, "What's it like here?"

Ramona: "My stomach relaxed. My jaw relaxed and my heart feels warmer."

Me: "Cool. Now tell me what kinds of things you will do, now that you know the truth of your future?"

"I'll just go and find my clients."

"Oh really? How?"

"I'll talk to people. I'll tell them that I'm a coach. I'll get clearer about how I can help them. I'll organize the workshops and I'll lead them. I will do the work and I will make it happen in its own time!"

The following week she had 3 paying clients.

Commitment as a Business Strategy

Having a plan B is understandable when you're going into an entrepreneurial adventure and you're doubting yourself, so you're not entirely sure if it's going to work financially. You have real bills to pay and real responsibilities that you need to uphold. The paradox is that when you have a plan B, your doubts will creep in much faster, and you will default to it whenever things start to get shaky, instead of continuing to stand in your commitment and adjusting your tactics.

If you talk to any successful coach (or dancer, or chef, or CEO), I *guarantee* that they will tell you that at some point, at some moment, they made the decision to stick with it and succeed even against the odds and in the face of their own doubts and fears.

I made this decision on the third day of my first coach training class. You probably made it at a different moment, and if you haven't made that decision yet I would encourage you to do it *if in fact* you do feel that it is your calling in life to do this work. If you think being a solopreneur is an easy way to quick fame and fortune, then you will find out very quickly how wrong you are. And if you want a career that's comfortable, do not become a life coach.

My commitment was challenged over and over again when clients wouldn't show up to appointments and when my income wasn't enough to support my needs. In 2008, I went from 35 clients to about 8 in the course of two months. But because I was committed, I got creative. I took my coaching practice to a high-end salon and convinced the owner that what he needed was an in-house coach for his clients. We tried it for a year and... it really wasn't working. Women were coming to the salon to *escape* their lives for a few delicious hours, not to face their deepest dreams and fears. I was seeing maybe one or two clients a week.

I remember one afternoon sitting in my gorgeous empty office with chandeliers and spotless $2,000 rugs and losing my shit. I was crumpled in fetal position and sobbing at what truly felt like a horrible mistake. But then there was a critical moment where, instead of listening to my ego (which was pummeled), I tuned in to my soul.

I started saying, "Thank you, God" over and over. My spirit knew that this situation, however painful, was developing me for something greater, and giving me valuable feedback about the direction in which I was going. I committed to coaching even more deeply and changed my course – I gave my notice that week. A warrior must be willing to "fail" and, to take responsibility, and to keep going.

Right now you are digging deep into the commitment of a warrior because you are learning how to be a coach *and* you are learning how to build a business. Give yourself the time to do this. Fall on your face and stay anyway. Do it for yourself because you know it's your soul's calling, and do it for your clients who need you.

Going All In

Have you ever gone canoeing? There is a moment when you have to push the canoe out into the water so that it's not stuck on the ground and it's actually very awkward. You've got one foot in the canoe and one foot out and it's very uncomfortable.

The current is pulling on the canoe so it's hard to pull it back to land, but you're also not fully in the canoe and enjoying the ride. This is what it's like to be halfway in with your business. It's awkward and uncomfortable. It's when you view coaching as a hobby or a side-hustle instead of a full-time gig where you are the founder and president.

The thing is that when you finally push off and get both feet into the canoe – and fully into your business – the wobbling stops. The current pulls you forward. You grab the oar and start rowing because you made the choice to be all in. Even if the damn thing tips over, you can swim to shore and flip it and climb back in.

Let's Make it Real

Take a piece of paper and write at the top, "I know I want to be a coach, but I'm not sure if I'm going to succeed at it."

Then I want you to write down how that feels, and what kinds of actions (or inactions) you would take from this perspective.

Now flip the paper over and write at the top, "I know that I am meant to be a coach and I know that my success is guaranteed."

How does it feel here? This is the place of the courageous and faithful warrior. Consider this your reality and write down the kinds of attitudes and actions (and inactions) you would take from this place.

It probably includes a whole lot more connecting with potential clients and a whole lot less working on perfecting your business cards.

It probably includes a whole lot more designing an amazing program that will serve your ideal client, and a whole lot less putting it off until tomorrow because, "Who knows if it will work anyway?"

It probably includes a whole lot more feeling relaxed and confident about the journey, and a whole lot less feeling like an anxious fraud.

This is what we want. This is who you were born to be.

Let's go. All in.

COURAGE

"Answering your call and living on your terms happens through action driven by a particular mindset and heartset, and it's strengthened by connecting deep within to what you and only you are called to be and do."

–RON RENAUD, *UNCOMPROMISED: WHEN YOU'RE READY TO LIVE YOUR LIFE ON YOUR TERMS*

Building a coaching business is not always easy. Ease and joy and creativity and fun are absolutely a part of the process, but I'm not going to lie to you and say that you won't experience any hardship in the process. In the face of this hardship however, you still and always have choices.

You are still in the realm of, "What do you really want?" This question is sometimes thrilling, sometimes terrifying, but almost always confronting because it is by design implying that whatever it is you really want, you *get to have it and it is your responsibility* to choose it.

There are many things we cannot choose or control. We cannot choose the color of our skin. We cannot choose when we or our loved ones will die. We cannot choose to avoid natural disasters. But there are limitless choices we can make about how we will respond to our lives. Even not choosing is a choice.

Are you choosing to respond to your life and to building your business with courage and creativity? Or are you responding with apathy and fear? This is the real work of the warrior coach. And here's another surprise: along with the thrill and delight of your wild success – financially and otherwise – will be moments of total terror about that success. Bringing our pipe dreams into the earthly realm will trigger fear. And the bigger the dream, the greater the doubts. There is no finish line in this work. As soon as you reach the top of one mountain, you will be compelled to climb to the next one (but please at least celebrate and enjoy the view for a good long while!).

The Joy and Terror of Wild Success

Last week I led a coach training for 550 top leaders at a large health care organization in New England. I jumped at the chance because this was my dream made manifest! For years I had been envisioning myself as a keynote speaker and coach trainer for business leaders. And here it was – served up on a warm plate with gravy. My heart leapt with excitement!

As soon as I said yes, I waited for the terror to arrive because – even though I was doing the thing that I said I always wanted to do – it was still something I had never done: A larger audience than I was used to, in a format that was unfamiliar (seven groups were watching via video conference and I had to put my thoughts into a PowerPoint... not usually how I roll).

Sure enough, two nights before the presentation I had my first anxiety dream where the audience was staring at me blankly and I was losing my words. In the morning, I started questioning the entire framework, myself, and my capabilities.

"They're not going to get it. I don't have what it takes."

"I'm a fraud anyway. I've never even been a director or above, who am I to be teaching them about leadership?"

"That exercise I put into the presentation is going to be a disaster."

"I'm too fat. They won't listen to me because I'm too goofy. And I'm too sensitive."

As you move toward your dreams of building a successful coaching business, I really encourage you to expect the terror and the doubts that will come along with the joy and excitement. Create space for them in your heart and your mind. Build a mansion for your doubts and fears and let them get comfortable. This is courage. Courage is not moving forward *without* fear, it's experiencing the fear and moving forward anyway.

It's much easier to live in the land of potential. "I *could be* such a great coach..." "I *could* write the best book..." "I could be such a success..." Living in the land of potential is very satisfying for the ego because it keeps the vision (and the work) out there somewhere – without the nervous sweat rings, the stumbling over your words, the pit of fear in your stomach as you actually dare to bring it from idea to earth.

To move towards your potential and test it out in the real world is an act of true warriorship.

Courage as a Business Strategy

I could easily choose to suffer my way through the writing of this book by thinking, "This is so confronting. Who will even want to read this? I bet I can think of all the ways my critics will tear this apart. I'm writing on a Saturday afternoon – what a crazy workaholic I am...."

But instead I'm choosing, "How cool is it that I get to write on a Saturday afternoon. Just by honoring my calling, I'm inspiring others. My book wants to be written. I'm so lucky that I am passionate about teaching and learning and the written word. If it all goes to hell, I'll still have my wonderful family. They won't care."

Keep it light and keep creating. Your journey will become more enjoyable, and as an extra bonus, your business will grow by leaps and bounds. And I'm going to say it again and again... no one is obsessing about your life, your journey, and your coaching as much as you are.

Find Your Buoys

Many of us, women in particular, tend to isolate when we are down in a hole. This is not helpful although I know when I'm in the hole it seems to make sense. But I have identified three anchors – actual people in my life – that I have an agreement with. They have agreed to meet me when I'm in the hole and encourage me out of it when I'm good and ready. I have agreed to do the same for them.

Virtual connections may not be quite as powerful as the real thing, but I must say, I have been uplifted time and time again through a Facebook comment or chat. There is a tribe of people who want to see you succeed and who will be cool with you when things aren't going well. One of my tribes is Megan Jo Wilson & The Army of Light on Facebook, and I hope you'll join us there. We've got your back.

Let's Make it Real

What do you really want?

Start asking yourself this question every day, and more importantly, answer it honestly. What do you *really* want? Write it down. Be courageous. The word courageous comes from Old French *corage* meaning "heart or innermost feelings." Listen to your heart and dare to answer this question each and every day.

What you really want may not always look like speaking in front of 550 corporate leaders. Sometimes it is to take a day to yourself to rest. Sometimes you want to invest in a training program that you know would feed your heart, mind, and spirit. Sometimes doing less is the most courageous act of all. Write it down and commit to making it real today.

GRACE

"Grace is energy infused with a force greater than our own... it illuminates your path by moving through your intuition, influencing the choices you make."

–CAROLYN MYSS, *INVISIBLE ACTS OF POWER*

I am not a theologian. I am not a pastor or a priest. I cannot tell you about world religions, or describe the different church denominations in my very own city. What I know about religion could probably be written in one sentence and would sound something like, "Religion is man's way of creating rules around the greatest mystery on earth. This has caused a lot of committed tribes, and a lot of problems."

So while I don't know much about religion, I do know about what I call grace and so do you if you're a coach. You are an alchemist after all, working in the great and mysterious field of transformation. So much of what you do is invisible and indescribable. It is magical in the truest sense of the word and it's why you often struggle to describe what you do as a coach.

What is Grace?

How can I articulate something so mysterious!? Well, since I brought it up, I'd better try. I would say that grace is divine energy with a purpose. It has a directive for us that is always pointing to our best learning, our best life, our highest good, and our most divine path. It surrounds us all the time, though we often ignore it.

I sometimes think of grace as a glowing energy – often just an inch or two in front of my feet, my mouth, my thoughts, tugging me toward my own divine expression.

If you are a child of the 80s, you remember Toucan Sam... "Just follow your nose! It always knows!" This is the image of grace for me – an invisible but powerful rainbow smell of divine direction that will pull you to where you are called to be moment by moment, month by month, year by year.

Grace is always there to guide you and you know this. You have experienced it yourself when you felt an urge, big or small, responded to it, and noticed the most unusual coincidences beginning to appear. This is divine synchronicity, and for many of us who believe in it, it is a matter of law, not luck.

Most of us feel comfortable using the name "God" in the big moments of life (weddings and funerals, for example), but for the sake of your life as a coach in business, I'm talking about the daily direction from the divine: The grace that will direct you in every moment as you are connecting with a new client.... The grace that will compel you to lead an afternoon meeting in an entirely new way, or reach out to a new connection on a hunch.... The grace that will pull you into a shop you've never walked into before, even when you're running late, only to find there's an opportunity there that perfectly serves your purpose.

The energy of grace will often pull us in directions that don't make logical sense, and this makes some of us uncomfortable. We are a logical people here in U.S. of A. after all. We look at the data. We make pros and cons lists. We sit behind desks in fluorescent-lit conference rooms with our paper cups of black coffee and make a case for elaborate strategic initiatives for the next ten years that are based on facts, logic, and complex models of projected income.

There is nothing wrong with logic, in fact it is one of my favorite life-long companions. But it can truly get in the way of divine beckoning. When we begin to follow God's grace with trust, the most outrageous and unexpected outcomes will begin to show up in our lives, and this is not familiar in a culture that prefers to have five and ten year plans and a sense of control.

Sometimes the pace of grace moves faster than we are able to handle it in our current mental and emotional state. This is why it can take us 8 years to leave our soul-sucking jobs even when *we know* on another level that it's time to move on. We battle the guidance saying things like, "It's not that bad. I need this income for my responsibilities. My parents will give me grief if I leave my job...." We sometimes ignore the direction of grace because although it is always for our good, it is often outrageous, illogical, and therefore more than a little confronting!

How Can I Listen to Grace?

Divine grace is always moving within us and around us. It draws us towards some people and opportunities, and will strongly guide us away from others, if only we will "listen" and respond. It is a sense, a knowing without knowing, a vision you can't seem to shake, a sense of inspiration, a calling, a deep desire.

My client Keisha is an amazing example of a woman who is tethered deeply to her relationship to grace. She is also a very practical business strategist. She had a clear vision of starting her own company with other like-minded magical humans, and together we articulated her purpose which was (and is) to awaken magic in others even and especially in boardrooms and cubicles.

She also got clear that she didn't want to lead this vision on her own. She started to consider potential partners and not surprisingly, the partner appeared shortly after. This partner was bright and bold and like Keisha, she was also on a mission to bring humanity and magic into the workplace, so they began to meet regularly to develop the plans.

During one of our coaching sessions, she told me how quickly things were moving forward and I said, "This is truly worth celebrating! What are you most excited about!?"

The line went quiet and I could feel her energy sinking.

"You know what?" she said, "I'm not excited."

This was a surprise for both of us, so we took the time to explore it. She couldn't point to something specific that wasn't working – in fact, everything looked just fine on paper. There was no evidence or data that would support the idea of "This is not the right partner," but grace was there whispering in her ear, "This is definitely not it."

To Keisha's credit, she shared her feelings honestly with her partner who admitted she was also feeling the same way! They had learned through the process that they wanted to lead autonomously and with different outcomes. They amicably parted ways, even though there was no plan B. The plan A that Keisha had invested time, money, and energy into was gone. But she had faith and trusted her decision to respond to grace.

What happened next? About a week later, she learned about a CEO opening at another company. Grace was stirring her and once again, she responded. Although the CEO position would mean working for another organization, she realized right away that this was an opportunity completely aligned with her purpose, although wrapped in an unexpected package. Three months later, we were celebrating her new role as CEO.

"I never thought I would find myself here," she said. "And it's perfect."

Tuning in to Grace

As warrior coaches, we must become attuned to the grace in our own lives. How does divine grace want to use us next? What about right now? What is the direction we are called to go in this moment, and this moment, and this moment? When we tune in, we slide into the current of an adventure that will always bring us exactly what we need.

Grace was leading the way when I left my newborn baby for a week and spent $4,000 I didn't have. (This is how I was hired as a faculty trainer for CTI – a dream I had held for ten years.)

Grace was leading the way when I said no to a huge scholarship to get a Master's Degree in Creative Writing at American University so that I could meditate in the woods. (This is how I became a black belt in martial arts, a decision that has saved my life literally and spiritually on more than one occasion.)

Grace was leading the way when I said yes to quitting my corporate job to move to Spain. (This is how I learned a second language, and stepped into my unique expression as a leader.)

Grace was leading the way when I refused to have surgery or give up on having kids, even though every gynecologist I'd ever met with said it would be nearly impossible. (This is how I conceived within a week, had a flawless pregnancy, and a perfectly healthy daughter who is the love of my life.)

Do your best to respond in alignment with the information you are being given from heaven. If you are getting strong messages to do (or not do) something, and you're sure that the messages are coming from divine will, it will serve you to act on them as quickly as possible. *This* is faith and this is where "success" lives, brave soul. This is the path to your dreams, and this is what our clients want more of in their own lives. Are you willing to be a living and breathing model of bold faith?

Grace and Faith as a Business Strategy

Do you have faith in yourself as a coach? Do you have faith in your business? The Bible says, "Faith is the substance of things hoped for, the evidence of things not seen." (Hebrews 11:1) This verse is pointing to, not just the vision of your business – which is the substance – but the *unshakable* knowing that it shall come to pass. Do you see the substance of the things you hope for? Do you see evidence of things that you cannot see with your eyes?

Do you operate from a sense of knowing your own success as if it were as real as evidence in a court case? *That's* the kind of crazy faith we're talking about, and that's the kind of crazy faith that has led to every successful and good thing in my life.

Crazy unshakable faith will respond to the guidance of grace and will keep you from settling for less because you know something even better is on the way.

Crazy unshakable faith will respond to the guidance of grace and keep you moving forward from a place of relaxed knowing, instead of anxiety and desperation.

Imagine if you approached every potential client *knowing beyond the shadow of any doubt* that you are and shall be a successful coach. It will not always be easy to stay in this place of unshakable faith, but it is the best place to put your energy. Lean into this crazy faith whenever possible. Why?

Because faith and fear cannot operate together. As soon as you step into one, you are stepping out of the other. So like anything else, there is a choice to be made. Will I move forward with this faith that is based on evidence of things I can't even *see*?! If the alternative is staying stuck in fear then I say, "Fuck yes, I choose faith."

If nothing else, responding to grace with faith will get you into inspired action. None of us truly knows what the future holds, but I notice that people who act like they know they are going to succeed in the future – guess what? Those are the people who succeed.

So act like you know. Move through the world as if there is nothing to be afraid of and watch how the waters part. Walk through your day as if your success is absolutely guaranteed and you will see mountains of fear crumble to the ground. Your enemies internal and external will vanish like vampires in the sun, and the opportunities to work with paying clients will begin to swarm around you like honey bees to a hive.

Why not try it anyway? I always say that I don't care if God is real, or not. I truly do not. If I die and that's it – well, then that's it. But in the meantime, I get to live in a way that is magical and inspiring, and that gives me real comfort in times of despair. God is real to me and even if it's all a trick my human brain is playing, then I'm signed up for the trick for life because it makes me feel better and it gets me better results. Why would I choose anything else?

Let's Make it Real

What helps *you* to connect with divine grace? Is it music? Writing? Meditation? Prayer? Dancing like a wild-woman in your living room? Making a bonfire and ceremoniously burning the thoughts that no longer serve you? There are many ways to connect to divine grace. Find the one that works for you and make it a daily habit so that you defer more often to your soul's deep knowing about *your* version of wild success as a coach.

Affirm who you are and what's possible. Declare out loud:

I am divinely guided at all times.

My success is a total guarantee.

Every time I feel like I'm falling down a hole, I know that God is there to catch me and lift me higher.

The perfect clients are coming my way in a perfect way under God's grace.

I am a divine conduit for money energy. Money is good because I use money for good.

Now write some of your own affirmations and read them every morning and every night this week. Or forever.

A faithful inner world will always translate into faithful action in the outer world.

The primary sound of prayer is "thank you."

The primary response to grace is "yes."

Let's pray.

A Prayer for the Warrior Coach

Great and powerful God, Source of Creation, Unlimited Universal Love, in your mercy, hear my prayer.

As I turn my attention to your divine presence, I can feel the sacred gift of this very moment, and I say thank you. Thank you for another day. Thank you for another opportunity to learn and grow. Thank you for the breath in my body, the thoughts in my mind, and the inspiration of my spirit. Thank you for this very moment.

God, you have called me to do work that transforms lives. You have gifted me with a heart that loves and listens. You have touched my spirit in a way that inspires me to touch the lives of others. I see that this is a unique gift, and I ask that you guide me now as I move forward on this path.

How would you have me be used? Help me to hear you, see you, and feel you at every step. Help me to move according to your will in a perfect way through grace.

I trust you and I ask that you help me to trust you more. I trust myself and I ask you to help me to trust myself more. I welcome your divine light into my life right now. I welcome your divine light into my thoughts and I ask that you clear away anything that does not support your will for my purpose. Clear away my doubts and fears like only you can.

Fill me with courage as I learn what needs to be learned. Help me to be bold in the name of serving others. Help me to love and accept myself right where I am and then guide my feet to where I should go next with my work. Bless my path and bless the paths of those who are seeking me.

What I am seeking is now seeking me, and for that I am grateful.

Thank you for this day. Thank you for this gift of life. Let your will be done.

Amen.

WHAT'S NEXT

"There is actually a very thin line between what we have and what we want."

–MIKE BORNHORST, LICSW, CPCC, PCC

In case you didn't catch this yet, let me summarize:

You will stumble.

You will shine.

You will lose faith.

You will find your faith deepening.

You will make mistakes.

You will be brilliant.

You will lose track of your fulfillment and what really matters to you.

You will be deeply aligned with and inspired by your life.

You will get depressed and think that you're crazy for wanting to start a coaching business when you can't even get a grip on your own life.

You will know without a doubt that building this business is what you were born to do.

Your ego will compare yourself to other coaches and entrepreneurs who are "ahead" of you in the game. This will make you feel like a loser and wish that you had a more colorful lipstick in your purse even though you don't wear lipstick or carry a purse.

Another part of you will become desperate to know *how* the story is going to end and wish that there was a linear path that would guarantee your success.

If you're not mindful, you will spend your time and money in the wrong places and you won't charge what you're worth, and then you'll have to find a part-time job to pay for your real financial life. Then that part-time job will turn into a full-time job.

What's Next?

Hire a coach.

This is deep work. Hire a coach you love that will reconnect you over and over and over to your own amazingness so that you can do the rest. You are a truly powerful person. It's just that sometimes you forget. We all do. Hire a coach to keep you there.

If you so believe in this magical work, then you should be investing in a coach for yourself. Your clients will show up the same way that you do.

Find your tribe.

Along with an individual coach, find groups of like-minded people that you can lean into in challenging times. This is easier than ever with social media sites that will do the algorithmic work for you.

I have also created my own tribe of warrior coaches. We learn together. We meet online and gather at live retreats. You can be a part of this tribe, too. There is nothing more powerful than finding a tribe in which you belong. Go to my Facebook Group, "Megan Jo Wilson & The Army of Light."

Decide what matters more.

Claim it now: What matters more than the obstacle? What matters more than looking good? What matters more than perfection? (Please answer this question and post it in my Facebook Group, Megan Jo Wilson & The Army of Light!)

My "what matters more" is connecting coaches to the leaders they were born to be. What really helps me get over myself is watching the news for about 30 seconds. I know it is only telling a fraction of the reality of the world, but what I see lights me on fire.

There is so much anger and fear and ignorance running the show outside our windows, it's a wonder we have the courage to move forward through our day.

And while coaching is (at the moment) primarily an industry of white privilege, it is slowly spreading outside of those boundaries.

Coaching gives us a way of being with ourselves and others that I believe is supporting our human evolution – our ability to be curious with one another. To open our minds to one another. To be able to be with our pain and our fury, and turn it into something useful rather than unleashing it on our family, our churches, our community, our country.

If I can inspire even a handful of the brilliant coaches I know to step out more boldly and connect with the clients – the nurses, the teachers, the parents, the middle-managers, the artists – who could so benefit from this work, then that's worth it.

CONCLUSION

YOU ARE A REAL FUCKING COACH!

The primary work in building a coaching business starts on the inside and knowing for yourself that *you* are already – right now – a real coach.

For better or for worse, we must be constantly buttressing a sense of esteem for ourselves so that we can show up and shine for our clients. We must be grateful for where we are while aiming for the stars. If we are asking our clients to be courageous, we must dare to be courageous ourselves. Not fearless. But moving forward in partnership with our fear – which will always show up, since we are in the business of evolution and transformation.

To be a coach is to be all in and totally committed to a life of inspiration, joy, and fulfillment, even when it means we disappoint others. Even when it means going against the values that have been passed down through our history. Even when it means facing our own demons that scream, "This is not realistic, you crazy woman!"

We must dance with the energy of grace and learn how to respond to it intuitively and creatively rather than reactively. We must be deeply connected to ourselves and vulnerably connected and exposed in front of others.

This is warriors' work. This is not the normal middle-of-the-road path. This is for magical humans like you who are willing to dive deep and say yes to all of it – the mess, the shaky legs, the sweaty armpits, the clients who don't sign up, and the challenge of writing a god-forsaken bio for our website.

Above all, I promise that it's so worth it. When we commit to a life of fulfillment and inspiration… when we are connected to our spiritual purpose and the grace that guides us… when we anchor ourselves to supportive partners and tribes, we become magnetic to the clients we wish to serve.

Also we get to have a hell of a ride.

"Make every breath count," was my mentor Art's dying wish. That is my wish for you. That you wake up every day knowing that your life matters and that you are honoring the way in which you are called to serve.

My wish for you is that you respond to that call with as much grit and grace as you can possibly muster because you know that by doing so, you are changing the course of the planet for the better.

My wish for you is that you lighten up and love the playful magic of coaching. That you give yourself a break from having to be brilliant every session. That you listen with deep presence, you reconnect people to what matters, and you hold them lovingly accountable to it. Can you hear how valuable that is?! Can you feel how much all of us need this kind of listening at this point in human history?

My wish is that you know you are not alone. If you are anxious, terrified, hesitant, or any version of "not quite ready," my wish is that you know you are not alone and you are not a wimp. This is what I *really* want to help you with.

Come play with us.

The first thing I'd love for you to do is to join my tribe "Megan Jo Wilson & The Army of Light" on Facebook. You will be met with encouragement and support. This is a place where you can share your successes and failures, resources and practical ideas with other like-minded magical warrior humans.

My mission is to build this army of light through coaching, with as many brigades and platoons as I can possibly handle, and then some more on top of that. For some of you, reading this book is all you need to shift your approach. You are doing the exercises and making it happen on your own. I say awesome and amen.

For others of you, this book has been a doorway into understanding that there is something golden in this process, and that pulling it off on your own is a little bit more daunting than you imagined. You are the ones I want to work with most. If you want support in walking through this process by working directly with me, and connecting to other magical humans who are learning with you, please go to **www.meganjowilson.com** so that we can make some time to talk one-on-one.

I'll end with this passage from *Conversations with God (Book 2)* by Neale Donald Walsch:

"Bless the Process, and accept it as the greatest gift to the Kindest Creator. Embrace the Process, and move through it with peace and wisdom and joy. Use the Process, and transform it from something you endure to something you engage as a tool in the creation of the most magnificent experience of All Time: the fulfillment of your Divine Self."

FURTHER READING

The Secret Door to Success – Florence Scovel-Shinn

Anatomy of the Soul – Carolyn Myss

Pussy: A Reclamation – Regena Thomashauer

Loving What Is – Byron Katie

The Places That Scare You – Pema Chodron

The Hero's Journey – Joseph Campbell

Conversations with God: An Uncommon Dialogue – Neale Donald Walsch

Co-Active Leadership: 5 Ways to Lead – Henry Kimsey-House, Karen Kimsey-House

The Soul of Money: Reclaiming The Wealth of our Inner Resources – Lynne Twist

ACKNOWLEDGMENTS

I start by giving all thanks and praise to the Master Creator, the great mystery, and the source of all things. Goddess. Universe. Source. Light.... Whatever we call you, I know you to be real and awesome. Thank you, God.

Thank you Angela Lauria, my brilliant editor, publisher, coach, and marketing genius all wrapped up into one. I heard the call that it was time to write a book and BOOM – there you were. Of course.

In good times and bad, I have always *always* reached for a book. So, I give a deep and grateful bow to Florence Schovel-Shinn, Carolyn Myss, Martin Luther King, Jr., Pema Chodron, Audrey Lorde, Byron Katie, Debbie Ford, Kate Northrup, Wayne Dyer, Christiane Northrup, Brené Brown, Agnes Sanford, Deepak Chopra, Louise Hay, William Sloane Coffin, Lynn Twist – and Joseph Campbell, who said, "My meditation is underlining sentences." To that I say... Amen!

As a Co-Active Coach I am a proud member of a truly mighty tribe that wraps around the globe and gives me hope that we might just survive as a species. All who are a part of this tribe are kindred spirits. Co-Active was created by my colleagues Henry Kimsey-House, Karen Kimsey-House, and Laura Whitworth. You are wonderful geniuses. Thank you for changing the course of my life forever.

This book would not exist without my Co-Active mentors and friends: Art Shirk, Elaine Jaynes, Hide Enomoto, Eric Kohner, Mike Bornhorst, Pat House, Ken Mossman, Sam House, Ron Renaud, L.A. Reding, Rick Tamlin, Milne Kintner, Hope Langner, Jim Patterson, Susan Carlisle, Deborah Colman, and Christie Mann. (At this point I am just sobbing because it's absurd how totally blessed I am when I put it down in writing.)

To my Co-Active Leadership Turtle tribe of Spain: What a bunch of brilliant weirdos we are! Thank you for fanning the flames of my eccentricity and danger. Ho.

A deep bow to The Riverview Foundation School of Martial Arts and to Sifu Atripaldi who saved my life by teaching me that my life was worth saving. Thank you for holding up a mirror to my inner warrior.

Thank you to my wonderful parents who are truly the most intelligent and interesting people I know! My mother Joyce Wilson-Sanford, for showing me that work can be interesting and joyful. (You're a real hoot!) And to Don David Sanford, the Great Appreciator who raised me to stay in awe in the presence of rocks, ocean, and moss.

Thanks to my dad, Rick Wilson, who has dedicated his life to international human rights and who brought me to Bogota, Colombia when I was 13. Thank you for opening my mind to the total thrill of new cultures and of being able to order a hamburger in Spanish.

And to Kate Cauley – my WOMI (Woman of Maternal Influence) – who has been my cheerleader every step of the way, encouraging me, creating beauty and order, and asking the very best questions over dinner and great wine. You uplift me at every turn.

Sara Hallie Richardson, you inspire me. You uplift me. You crack me up like none other! This is our new normal. #whatarewegonnawear

To my pastor, Kenneth I. Lewis, thank you for keeping me grounded in scripture, and for teaching about Christ's Kingdom in ways that make me think and laugh and stand up and yell, "Yassss!"

To my only daughter, Issa. You are my master teacher and the greatest miracle of my life. Thank you for showing me what pure curiosity and kindness looks like. I am with you always dear Bubbie. And to her father, Joshua Hughes, your prayers, encouragement, and endless schedule shuffling mean the world to me! Thank you for believing in me.

And to the love of my life, Matt Day. I don't know how this happened, but somehow, I found you and it is beyond everything I ever dreamed of. Thank you for making space for me to be terribly distracted while I organized chapters in my head. This book would not have been written without you. I love you and I know it.

ABOUT THE AUTHOR

Megan Jo Wilson is a coach, author, mom, and professional singer based in Portland, Maine. She supports new coaches in launching wildly successful businesses through spiritual entrepreneurship and what she calls, "The Warrior's Way."

Since her first Co-Active Coaching course in 2004, she has been committed to spreading the power and magic of Co-Active through coaching and coach training.

She is a Certified Professional Co-Active Coach (CPCC), a faculty Coach trainer at the global leadership development organization CTI, and a black belt in Martial Arts at Riverview Foundation of Maine.

An artist and professional performer, Megan Jo stands firmly in her belief that "There is nothing more expensive than boredom." She partners with business leaders and organizational teams to support them in expanding creativity, engagement and authentic leadership in the workplace through coaching.

Some of her many passions include: homemade soup, underground hip hop, reading in bed, building fires, enormous earrings, and the desert of Morocco.

Website: **meganjowilson.com**

Email: **megan@meganjowilson.com**

Facebook: facebook.com/megan.j.wilson.90

Twitter: mjwcoaching

Facebook Group: Megan Jo Wilson & The Army of Light

THANK YOU

Hello, brave soul,

Thank you for reading. The fact that you've gotten to this point in the book tells me something important about you: You're committed and you're ready to go all in on building a coaching business that changes lives – your own included!

CONTACT ME: I'd love to hear more about your coaching and the impact you dream of having with your coaching business.

Please email me at **megan@meganjowilson.com** or find me on Facebook at

https://www.facebook.com/megan.j.wilson.90

JOIN US: One of my fundamental beliefs is that we all need support and community in this crazy coaching journey. I invite you to join our amazing tribe of warrior coaches in our Facebook group "Megan Jo Wilson & The Army of Light."

LET'S TALK: If you are interested in setting up a one-on-one call with me, please go to **www.meganjowilson. com.** I can't wait to meet you!

HAVE A LISTEN: Do you love music? You can find my latest EP, "Tin" and my first record "Seed, Stars, Galaxies" on iTunes or at CDbaby.com. You will also find music by my 20-piece big band "The Fogcutters." Have a listen and tell me what you think!

Let's do this.

Xoxo

Megan Jo

difference press

Difference Press offers entrepreneurs, including life coaches, healers, consultants, and community leaders, a comprehensive solution to get their books written, published, and promoted. A boutique-style alternative to self-publishing, Difference Press boasts a fair and easy-to-understand profit structure, low-priced author copies, and author-friendly contract terms. Its founder, Dr. Angela Lauria, has been bringing to life the literary ventures of hundreds of authors-in-transformation since 1994.

LET'S MAKE A DIFFERENCE WITH YOUR BOOK
You've seen other people make a difference with a book. Now it's your turn. If you are ready to stop watching and start taking massive action, reach out.

"Yes, I'm ready!"

In a market where hundreds of thousands books are published every year and are never heard from again, all participants of The Author Incubator have bestsellers that are actively changing lives and making a difference.

"In two years we've created over 250 bestselling books in a row, 90% from first-time authors." We do this by selecting the highest quality and highest potential applicants for our future programs.

Our program doesn't just teach you how to write a book—our team of coaches, developmental editors, copy editors, art directors, and marketing experts incubate you from book idea to published bestseller, ensuring that the book you create can actually make a difference in the world. Then we give you the training you need to use your book to make the difference you want to make in the world, or to create a business out of serving your readers. If you have life-or world-changing ideas or services, a servant's heart, and the willingness to do what it REALLY takes to make a difference in the world with your book, go to http://theauthorincubator.com/apply/ to complete an application for the program today.

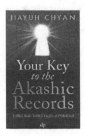